C000193608

IMAGES OF ENGLAND

Enderby, Narborough and Littlethorpe

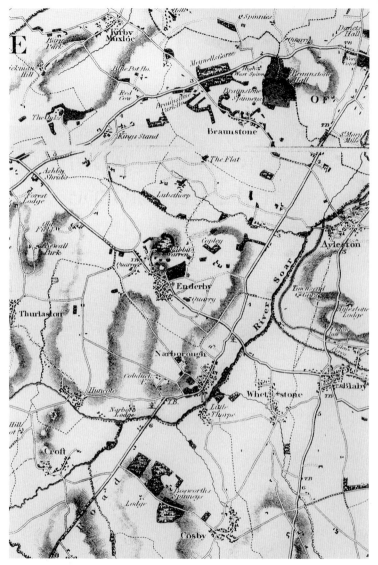

Greenwoods map of 1825, showing the villages of Enderby, Narborough and Littlethorpe. Interestingly, stone quarries are marked around Enderby with the Roman Fosse Way passing in a north-southwest line.

IMAGES OF ENGLAND

Enderby, Narborough and Littlethorpe

John Crofts and Nigel Moreton

NONSUCH

First published 1998
This new pocket edition 2005
Images unchanged from first edition

Nonsuch Publishing Limited
The Mill, Brimscombe Port,
Stroud, Gloucestershire, GL5 2QG
www.nonsuch-publishing.com

British Library Cataloguing in Publication Data.
A catalogue record for this book is available from the British Library.

ISBN 1-84588-145-1

Typesetting and origination by Nonsuch Publishing Limited
Printed in Great Britain by Oaklands Book Services Limited

Contents

Acknowledgements   6

Introduction   7

1. Streets and Buildings   9

2. Sports and Leisure   49

3. Wartime   65

4. Personalities   71

5. Schools and Churches   79

6. Special Occasions   93

7. Transport, Trade and Industry   107

Acknowledgements

The authors would like to thank the people of Enderby, Narborough and Littlethorpe who kindly lent photographs, postcards and other items. Special thanks go to: Wendy Warren – 'Vanished Views', Fred Drummond, Mr and Mrs D.G. North, The British Library, The Leicester Mercury, Leicestershire Museum and Record Service and Enderby Parish Council.

Introduction

In this book the authors have presented photographs and information depicting village life from around the turn of the century. This is not a definitive work but represents a compilation of scenes, people and events, recorded for posterity.

The villages of Enderby, Narborough and Littlethorpe lie some five miles south west of Leicester and, prior to 1800, their economy was based on an agricultural system. With the development of small cottage industries, like framework knitting and boot and shoe making, and its associated trades, many people worked from their homes and the villages became more dependent on industry than farming. By the 1870s the railway network connections were completed in the county, and together with the growing demand for better paving materials for city streets, the quarrying of stone took over as the dominant employer. The area was blessed by large outcrops of quality granites and quarries soon opened on Enderby Hill and at Narborough (Red Hill). By 1900 the Leicestershire quarries had established markets for their products of paving setts, kerbing and broken stone in London, and many of the expanding cities in the North. The Empire Stone works in Narborough also benefited from the close proximity of the quarries for its raw materials.

After 1945, following restructuring and numerous changes in ownership, many of the local quarries closed down, leaving only Enderby Warren operational. This quarry had, by the 1960s, become one of the largest producers of aggregates in the county. The quarry closed in 1967 and brought to an end nearly 100 years of quarrying in the area.

The last two decades have seen some significant changes in the development of the area. The quarries have been used as landfill sites and now have a variety of factories and businesses in their place. The old quarry railway link is now an established nature trail appropriately called Whistle Way, and connects Enderby with Narborough. The Enderby Town football ground and the Empire Stone Works land in Narborough are now small housing estates. The National School opposite Enderby church is now home to a business enterprise, and the headquarters of a large building society now occupies the site of the County mental hospital at Carlton Hayes.

The M1 and M69 motorways are in close proximity and form important links with the rest of the country. At junction 21 of the M1 motorway the out of town shopping development known as Fosse Park forms part of a larger complex that is gradually diminishing the 'green wedge' between the villages and Leicester.

As a consequence of this development there has been an inevitable increase in house building and problems with traffic. However, much of the original village centres still survive and can be recognised from the photographs in this book.

One

Streets and Buildings

Cross Street, Enderby, *c.* 1900, looking down towards the Methodist church. The building on the left is the original Co-operative Society shop.

High Street, formerly Church Street, Enderby, *c.* 1890. The Havelock Arms public house is on the left.

Blaby Road, Enderby, *c.* 1920, looking west towards the church.

Cross Street, Enderby, *c.* 1950, looking up towards the Nags Head public house.

Enderby National School and the High Street, *c.* 1900.

The Cross, Enderby, c. 1950, looking towards the New Inn. The building on the left was built originally as a gentleman's reading room.

The New Inn, Enderby, c. 1900. Notice the pub sign advertising 'Good stabling'.

Enderby village post office and draper's shop, at the corner of Cross Street and Townsend Road, c. 1910.

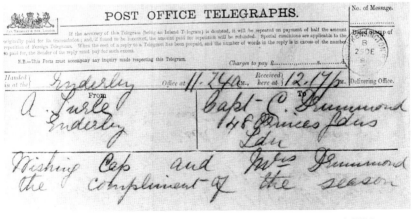

This is one of the first telegrams sent from Enderby post office. The message reads 'Wishing Captain and Mrs Drummond the compliments of the season, 25 December 1880'.

King Street, Enderby, *c.* 1890. There is a handcart carrying general hardware and the shop on the left sold tobacco, cigars and snuff.

King Street, Enderby.

King Street, Enderby, *c.* 1900, looking towards Rawson Street.

Marston House, standing on the corner of Hall Walk and Moores Lane, c. 1910. George Marston, one of the original local quarry-owners lived here before the turn of the century.

Hill House, Enderby. Here is a former vicarage, which stood on Mill Hill adjacent to the quarry workings. The great grandmother of Miss Young of West Street is on the back terrace. Croquet is being played on the house lawn.

Hall Walk, Enderby, *c.* 1900, looking towards the church. The wall surrounding Enderby Hall is on the left.

Enderby Hall, *c.* 1880.

Above: Enderby Hall, *c.* 1890. The lawns are being cut by horse drawn mower.

Right: A 'For Sale' notice, for Enderby Hall, Wednesday 7 June 1865. The Hall was purchased by Charles Brook Esq, of Yorkshire.

LEICESTERSHIRE.

Particulars and Plan
OF THE

ENDERBY HALL ESTATE,

CONSISTING OF

THE ANCIENT MANSION HOUSE CALLED

ENDERBY HALL,

With the Carriage Drives, Pleasure Gardens, Shrubberies, Walks, Conservatory, Vineries, Hothouses, Succession Pits, Orchard and Kitchen Gardens, Stabling, Carriage Houses, and other domestic offices;

The Manor or Lordship of Enderby,

With the Manorial Rights, Royalties, Wastes, Chief Rents, and Fishery;

The Impropriate Tithes,

The ADVOWSON of the Vicarage of ENDERBY cum WHETSTONE,

WATER CORN MILL AND MILLER'S COTTAGE,

GRANITE STONE QUARRY,

Two excellent FARM RESIDENCES, Eight COTTAGES and GARDENS, and

730 Acres, 3 Roods, 15 Perches of

VERY RICH AND SUPERIOR

Meadow, Pasture, and Arable Land,

SITUATE IN THE PARISHES OF

ENDERBY AND NARBOROUGH,

IN THE COUNTY OF LEICESTER.

To be Sold by Auction,

By Messrs. Cooke and Warner,

IN TWO LOTS,

At the BELL HOTEL, in LEICESTER,

ON WEDNESDAY, THE 7th DAY OF JUNE 1865.

Mill Lane, Enderby, *c.* 1918. The shop on the right is Spencer's drapers.

Keepers Lodge and the Warren, Enderby, *c.* 1918. The Lodge and Warren were on Harolds Lane leading to the vanished settlement of Lubbesthorpe.

The Cross, Enderby, c. 1918. The building on the left, constructed in 1872 and which is now the Conservative Club, was formerly the reading room and Working Men's Institute.

Cross Street, Enderby, c. 1905.

Enderby laundry on Hall Walk, *c.* 1900. Washing ladies pose outside the laundry.

King Street, Enderby, in 1905, looking towards Shortridge Lane.

The post office, Enderby, *c.* 1918. Enderby post office was run by Albert Lythall who also ran a firm of painters, decorators and plumbers.

Sarah Vann, standing outside her shop on the corner of Connery Lane and Mill Hill, Enderby, *c.* 1900. The sign advertises that the shop was licensed to sell beer but it was 'not to be consumed on the premises'.

Enderby Hall.

Above: Enderby Hall, date unknown.

Left: The Charles Brook Memorial in the playground of the National School. The National School, with a master's house attached, was built of local granite in 1860 and was enlarged in 1872 by Mr Brook. The school accommodated 200 children. Charles Brook was a wealthy Yorkshire mill owner who bought Enderby Hall in 1865 and went on to make a significant contribution to Enderby village. He paid for the rebuilding of the church in 1868 at a cost of £7,000, and was responsible for enlarging the National School at a cost of £500 in 1872. He also paid for the building of the reading rooms and Working Men's Institute which is situated on The Cross.

Mill Hill, Enderby, c. 1920. These quarry workers are outside the Plough public house.

The Plough Inn, 1980.

West Street, Enderby, looking south towards Carlton Hayes Hospital, *c.* 1918.

Sam Kilbys' shop on West Street, *c.* 1940.

Shortridge Lane, Enderby, *c.* 1925. Folly Cottages, on the right, were built in 1877. The King William IV public house is further down on the right.

A 1950s photograph of the King William IV public house, which was built in 1905.

Thatched 'cruck' cottages, Broad Street, Enderby. Built in the sixteenth century, they are now the premises of Barclays Bank.

W. Lakin hairdresser's and tobacconist shop, The Cross, Enderby, *c.* 1920.

The Webster's Old Forge, Mill Hill, Enderby, *c.* 1890.

High Street, Enderby, *c.* 1900. Children are out in their Sunday best to pose for the photographer.

Townsend Cottages, Enderby. In the distance is the chimney of the shoe works owned by the Co-operative Wholesale Society.

Newly built houses on Shortridge Lane, around 1925.

Bradshaw's grocery store, Cross Street, Enderby, *c.* 1960.

Looking down Cross Street, Enderby. The shop and cottages were demolished in the 1960s. The site is now occupied by Kwik Save supermarket.

The Pack Horse Bridge, Enderby, was built in the fifteenth century.

The Manor House, Hall Walk, Enderby. Originally dating from the fifteenth century, this timbered-framed house was later enlarged to its present size.

Fernleigh House, King Street, Enderby, *c.* 1950. Note the elaborate wrought iron railings running the whole length of the front.

Enderby village centre, *c.* 1960.

High Street, Enderby, *c.* 1918.

Chapel Street, Enderby, *c.* 1918. This scene looks towards the Congregational chapel which was built in 1849. The chapel housed a Sunday school and was used to house an African Mission and a library.

Shortridge Lane, Enderby, in 1970. Folly Cottages, on the right, were built in 1877 and demolished in the late 1970s.

A view across the gardens on Shortridge Lane looks towards King Street, in the 1940s.

A view of Enderby, showing the development of the village by 1986.

Opposite above: Carlton Hayes Hospital, c. 1980.

Opposite below: Carlton Hayes county mental hospital, standing in isolation in the 1930s.

The Narborough Hotel, Leicester Road, Narborough, *c.* 1920.

Coventry Road, Narborough, in 1960.

Main Street, Narborough, looking towards the village centre, in 1910.

Auburn Road, The Fosse, Narborough, in 1907. The building on the left was used as a convent.

The Blue Bell Inn, Narborough, in 1905.

Leicester Road, Narborough, looking north, *c.* 1910.

The post office, Narborough, on the corner of Park Road, around 1910.

Leicester Road, Narborough, *c.* 1900.

Narborough village, looking south.

A view of Narborough village from All Saints church tower, *c.* 1960.

The Rectory, Narborough, *c.* 1910.

Main Street, Narborough, *c.* 1910. The Narborough Arms public house is in the background. Note the handcart on the left, outside what is now a butcher's shop.

The Bell public house, Main Street, Narborough, *c.* 1980.

Main Street, Narborough, *c.* 1910. The village pump stands in the foreground to the right.

A Narborough street scene in 1904. The large building on the left is Narborough Hall.

Leicester Road, Narborough, c. 1910.

Narborough village, *c.* 1960.

Leicester Road, Narborough, *c.* 1960. Narborough House is the building the left. A Marsh and Butler van is delivering to the Bell Inn on the right.

Narborough Hall, *c.* 1960.

An aerial view of Narborough village, looking north, in 1960. All Saints church is to the centre right. The works at the bottom right are those of the Empire Stone Company.

The Square, Littlethorpe, *c.* 1900.

The Square in Littlethorpe, looking from the New Inn, *c.* 1900.

Station Road, Littlethorpe, looking towards Narborough in 1960.

A general view from Littlethorpe, c. 1950. The Yeoman's house is on the right.

Two

Sports and Leisure

Enderby Ladies hockey team, c. 1920.

A group of ladies at the Grand Bazaar and Sale of Work outside the old Ex-Servicemen's Social Club on Townsend Road, Enderby, c. 1950. They include Mrs Cooper, Mrs Wright, Mrs Cattel, Mrs Hutton, Mrs Brooks, Mrs Hall, Mrs Brown, Mrs Hunt, Mrs Sketchley, Mrs Lenton, Mrs Findley, Mrs Hulbert, Mrs Darley, Mrs Jayes Jnr, Mrs Belton, Mrs Jayes, Ida Edwards and Mrs Mellor.

Enderby Congregational chapel football team, in 1915.

The lads from Enderby football team in the 1950s.

Enderby football team, c. 1920.

Enderby Town football club, in 1915, after winning the Leicestershire Junior Cup and the Leicester and District League Championships. The club was founded by a group of local quarry workers in 1900. The secretary at the time was apparently an ardent Sunderland supporter who insisted the local team should also play in a red and white strip.

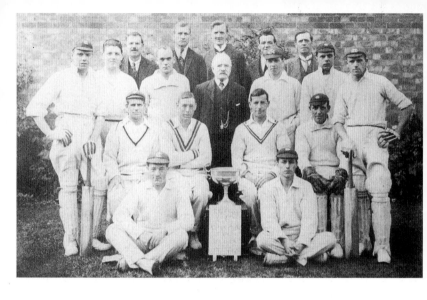

Above: Enderby cricket club, Champions of Division One of the South Leicestershire League, in 1925. These include T. W. Spence (Scorer), W. Carter (Secretary), F. Young, S. Coulson, W. Salt (Financial Secretary). Second row: A. Phillips, H. Young, E. Gilliver, T. Salt (President), W. North, W. Poyner, C. West, A. West, E. R. B Drummond, J. West (Captain) and H. Spence.

Left: The men's and women's team, outside Enderby cricket pavilion, Mill Lane.

A view across the cricket field between Bantlam Lane and Mill Lane, c. 1960.

A long standing resident, Arthur Capers MBE with Mr Fred Drummond at the cricket ground in 1986.

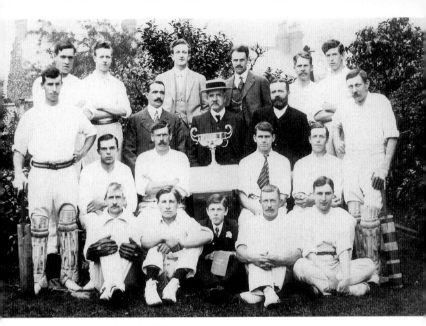

Enderby cricket club, Enderby in 1911.

Opposite above: Enderby Male Voice choir, in 1890.

Opposite below: Pictured here in 1947, are the Enderby and District Male Voice Choir, winners of the North Midland Championship. Included are Jack Underwood, Len Woofenden, Stan Barlow, Les Coulson, Alf Webster, Frank Dimmock, Gerald Illson, Wilf Mayne, Cliff Taylor, Eric Handley, Albert Charles, Ernest Robotham, Arthur Underwood, Sid Dilmore, Harold Farmer, Henry Shaw, Les West, Frank Price, Billy Brooks, George Chapman, Arthur Spence (pianist), Frank Burbett, Tommy Lenton, Dennis Humphrey, Eric Young (conductor), Major Pope (chairman), Jack Clark, Harry Brooks plus three unknown singers.

THE BROMLEY & DISTRICT MALE VOICE CHOIR,
WINNERS OF THE NORTH MIDLAND CHAMPIONSHIP
THE FLORENCE, LADY PAGET CHALLENGE SHIELD.

Enderby Village orchestra, pictured outside the National School, around 1900.

Right: A picture of Herbert Biggs, who was recorded as a boot maker in Kelly's Directory of 1912. He was a founder member of Enderby band.

Below: The Enderby town tand in parade uniform in 1931. Back row, left to right: Walli Ellis, Jim Phipps, Thomas Smith, -?-, Ernie Yeomanson, Dick Biggs, Walter Spence, Dick Ruder. Second Row: Albert Freestone, John Freestone snr, -?-, -?-, Bill John, William Freestone jnr, Eric Handy. Front row: Horace Geary, David Dickens, -?-, Jim Gilbert (conductor), Ernie Young, Bill Nibbs and Fred Seville.

Above: Enderby band on parade at the annual School Fête in Hinckley, in 1934.

Left: Job Biggs and his wife. Job was a founder member of the Enderby Band.

Right: Enderby band members, Ernie Yeomanson and Bernard Biggs, at Enderby Village Fête, *c.* 1940.

Below: Enderby band at the Village Hall, Enderby Village Fête, in the 1940s.

Above: Enderby band with their trophies, in 1936.

Left: Arthur Biggs in a quiet moment, after performing at Wicksteed Park.

Enderby town band, leading the British Legion on the Remembrance Day parade of Scouts and Guides, on Blaby Road, in the late 1960s.

The Remembrance Day parade, with the Enderby band, outside the Nags Head, Enderby, c. 1980.

Under direction by the Minister of Supply all unnecessary iron or steel railings, po
hains, bollards, gates, stiles, etc. in the Rural District of Blaby will shortly be
emoved and collected for use in the national war effort in iron and steel works and
oundries.

Notice is hereby given that on or after the 10th January, 1942 the work of removal w
ommence with the railings in the following parishes:- Aston Flamville, Blaby, Braunsto
osby, Countesthorpe Croft, Elmesthorpe, Enderby, Glenfields, Glen Parva, Huncote, Kil
irby Muxloe, Leicester Forest West, Narborough, Sapcote, Sharnford, Stoney Stanton,
hurlaston, Whetstone and Wigston Parva.

It is hoped that owners will be prepared to make a free gift of their railings, etc.
o the nation, but property owners and others whose interests are affected by the
emoval and who desire to claim compensation may obtain the appropriate form from:-
he Engineer & Surveyor, Council Offices, Narborough, near Leicester.

Under the provisions of the Compensation (Defence) Act, 1939, no claim for compensat
rdinarily can be entertained unless notice of claim has been given to the appropriate
uthority within a period of six months from the date of removal of the railings etc.

Under the provisions of Regulation 50, paragraph (3A) of the Emergency Powers (Defen
eneral Regulations no person shall be liable, by virtue of any obligation imposed by a
case or other instrument affecting the land or by or under any enactment or otherwise
o replace or provide a substitute for the thing severed, or to pay any sum by way of
amages or penalty or to suffer any forfeiture in consequence of a failure to perform
ny such obligation, and any person who has guaranteed the performance of any such
bligation shall be correspondingly relieved of his liability under the guarantee.

ouncil Offices,
  Narborough,   J. J. DERRY,
    Nr. Leicester.   Clerk of the Council.

1st December, 1941.

This was the notification for the removal of iron and steel railings, to be used in the war effort,
issued by Blaby Rural District Council, in December 1941.

Three

Wartime

C.FLIGHT.(NARBOROUGH) – 1461·SQUADRON – AIR·TRAINING·CORPS

– CHRISTMAS 1942. –

Narborough Air Training Corps, 1942. By this stage of the war all the three villages were well represented by the auxiliary forces.

Narborough Home Guard outside the rectory, Narborough, in 1940.

Enderby Girls Training Corps in 1940.

Wartime fire-service members in Enderby. Note the converted Morris, with its fire pump and wooden ladder.

The ARP outside Enderby Hall.

Enderby Company Home Guard, in 1940, showing off a Thompson machine gun and a Lewis gun.

The Enderby Division of the wartime fire service volunteers.

The Local Defence Volunteers, in the vicarage grounds, Enderby, *c.* 1940.

Four

Personalities

George Lowe, known in Enderby as 'Noggy', was the local chimney sweep in the early part of the century.

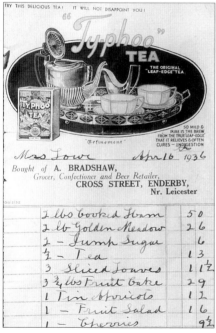

Above: The cottages opposite the Methodist church, 'Noggy' lived in the left-hand cottage. On the right of the picture is Mrs Lowe with a visitor. Beyond the cottages are the railings of the school which is now the village institute.

Left: An original bill of sale from Bradshaws' shop for 'Noggy' Lowes' funeral tea in 1936. It is interesting to note the prices!

Miss Mary Sloane, pictured on the left of her friend Miss Whittaker, in the garden of Sloane House. Mary Sloane was born in Leicester in 1867, where her father, John Sloane, was a local surgeon. She was educated at Belmont House school in New Walk, Leicester, and after a period at Leicester School of Art she went to the Royal College of Art in London. Her first exhibit was hung in the Royal Academy in 1896, and she was later to exhibit in all the major galleries in the country. In 1903, an etching of Aylestone Packhorse Bridge gained an honourable mention at the Paris Salon. Miss Sloane became a member of the Society of Women Artists in 1905 and was later a member of the Royal Society of Painter, Etchers and Engravers. She was to become great friends with William Morris (1834–1896), designer, poet and member of the Arts and Crafts Movement, and also his daughter May. Although Mary Sloane was not born in Enderby, she was happy to settle down here in later life with her companion and friend Miss Whittaker. She died in 1961 in her house in the Nook.

Miss Sloane's house was demolished in the 1960s and the site is now occupied by senior citizens' bungalows. Her name is still remembered in Sloane Close.

Opposite: The garden of Miss Sloane's house.

Miss Mary Sloane here, inside her home, in 1961, at the age of 91.

Local Enderby men pose for a photograph in 1920. Alf Webster, John Bryan and Bill West are in the party.

An Enderby family, c. 1890.

Frank Biggs, *c.* 1900. He was Enderby's village cobbler and lived in John Street.

Five

Schools and Churches

The Band of Hope, Narborough, *c.* 1900.

St John the Baptist's church, Enderby, during restoration, 15 May 1867. The tower was left intact, only the body of the church was rebuilt.

Right: A notice announcing the reopening of the church.

Below: The church, after the reopening in 1868.

Left: The interior of Enderby church, *c.* 1900. The inscription, which has now been painted over reads, 'Thou shalt worship the Lord thy GOD and Him only shalt thou serve'.

Below: Enderby church, with an inset of the vicar, Frewen Aylward, in 1910.

Above: Enderby church, viewed from High Street, *c.* 1940.

Right: The Revd A. Frewen Aylward, vicar of Enderby from 1884–1914.

A greetings card of Enderby church in winter.

Church & Vicarage, Enderby.

The church and vicarage of Enderby, looking across the grounds.

A group outside the vicarage in Enderby, c. 1900.

The annual fête in the grounds of the Enderby vicarage in 1983. The attractions included skittles, darts and the more general sales stalls.

Laying the foundation stones of the new congregational church on Thursday 15 July 1909.

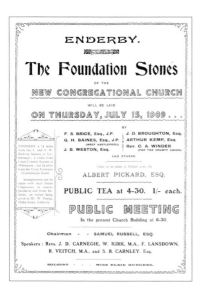

ENDERBY.

The Foundation Stones

OF THE

NEW CONGREGATIONAL CHURCH

WILL BE LAID

ON THURSDAY, JULY 15, 1909 . . .

BY

F. S. BRICE, Esq., J.P.   J. D. BROUGHTON, Esq.
G. H. BAINES, Esq., J.P.   ARTHUR KEMP, Esq
              (WEST HARTLEPOOL)
J. B. WESTON, Esq.   Rev. C. A. WINDER
                    (FOR THE COUNTY UNIONS).

AND OTHERS.

ENDERBY is 1½ miles   Chair to be taken at THREE p.m., by
from the L. and N.W.
Railway Station at Nar-
borough ; 2 miles from
Great Central Station at   ALBERT PICKARD, ESQ.
Whetstone ; and 3½ miles
from the Tram Terminus
(Narborough Road)   PUBLIC TEA at 4-30.   1/- each.

Arrangements can be
made with local Brake
Proprietors to convey   ## PUBLIC MEETING
parties to and from En-
derby, on notice being   In the present Church Building at 6-30.
given to Mr. W. Young,
(Baby Road), Enderby.

Chairman - - - SAMUEL RUSSELL, ESQ.

Speakers : Revs. J. D. CARNEGIE, W. KIRK, M.A., F. LANSDOWN,
R. VEITCH, M.A., and S. B. CARNLEY, Esq.

SOLOIST - - - MISS ELSIE BURGESS.

ENDERBY.

THE OPENING

OF THE

New Congregational Church,

ENDERBY, WILL TAKE PLACE ON

MONDAY, APRIL 25, 1910.

3 p.m., OPENING CEREMONY, presided over by

J. B. WESTON, Esq. (Leicester)

AN OLD SCHOLAR.

The Doors will be opened by

GERARD N. FORD, Esq. (Buxton)

3-30 p.m., Public Worship, Preacher:

Rev. J. D. JONES, M.A., B.D.

(of Bournemouth), Chairman Congregational Union of England and Wales.

5 p.m., PUBLIC TEA - - 1/- each.
COLLECTIONS FOR THE BUILDING FUND.

7 P.M., PUBLIC MEETING.

SPEAKERS :   Chairman - - - F. S. BRICE, Esq.
Rev. J. D. JONES, GERARD N. FORD, Esq., Rev. F. LANSDOWN,
SAMUEL RUSSELL, Esq. (Leicester), and the Pastor (A. Ewart Jones).
COLLECTIONS FOR THE BUILDING FUND.

SUNDAY, MAY 1st, at 10-45 and 6-15,

PREACHER : REV. DR. A. E. GARVIE

Posters advertising the stone-laying and the opening of the church.

The National School, High Street, Enderby, c. 1910.

The National Infants School in its commemoration year, 1897. The building is now the Enderby Village Institute.

Class at Enderby Church School, around 1900. The age of the photograph can be seen by its battered appearance.

Opposite above: Enderby Church of England school, senior class A, *c.* 1930.

Opposite below: The Infants school, Townsend Road, Enderby, *c.* 1925. Pictured here are Harold Rourke, Edwin Freer, Alan Freestone, Norman Egginton, Denis Elliott, Ken Moore, Wilf Farmer, ? Carter, George Brown, Billy Whitmore, Sidney Hudson, Hazel Orton, Phylliss Hales, Gladys White, Florence Cooper, Vera Coulson, Elsie Heggs, Alice Mollett, Dorothy Smith, Evelyn Palmer, Elsie Ruff and one other, name unknown.

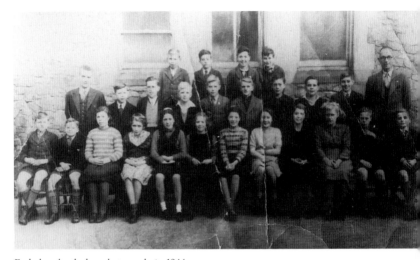

Enderby school, class photograph, in 1944.

Enderby school, c. 1940.

A class at Enderby school in the 1950s

Brockington College, Enderby, Class 11A, in 1960.

St John's church, Aldeby, c. 1920. This picture depicts a service probably commemorating the patron saint, celebrating St John the Baptist Day, which is 24 June.

Six

Special Occasions

'The Stallholders' at Enderby garden fête, July 1906. The fête was held in the grounds of Enderby Hall.

A group of prominent Enderby citizens, including Mrs G. Grace, Miss Aylward, Mrs F.R. Donisthorpe, Mrs Aylward, Mrs F.R. Donisthorpe, Revd A.J. Aylward, Miss Pudmore, Miss Grace, Miss Aylward, Miss Aylward, Miss Grave, Mrs H. Jayes, Miss S. Fox, Miss J. Fox, Mrs. Bigges, Mrs W. Butler, Mr H. G. Grace, Mrs E. Wright, Mrs G. Martin, Mrs W. Clarke, Mrs W. Salt, Mrs G. Salt, Mrs F. West, Mrs M.G. Spencer, Mrs J. Turton, Miss E. Taylor, Mrs F. Young, Mrs J. Borman, Mrs G. Young, Mrs F. Bennett, Mrs F. Mills, Mrs E. Hemmings, Mr C. Fox, Mr G. Biggs, Mr H. Cliffe, Mr W. Clarke, Mr J. Norton and Mr H. Biggs.

The Empire Stone Company orchestra, Narborough, *c.* 1930.

The players and orchestra, Narborough, *c.* 1930.

A street scene, outside William Lowes' shop in Connery Lane, Enderby, c. 1910.

The Cross, Enderby. The celebrations are possibly for the coronation of Edward VII, 9 August 1902. Note the army personnel outside the shop, waving flags saying 'God Save the King'.

Enderby Village centre celebrations, c. 1910.

An unknown group, c. 1900.

The Co-operative Society float, which was carrying biscuits and preserves outside the Enderby Co-operative Society Ltd old bakery, which was built in 1914. It now belongs to a fireplace company.

A group dressed in theatrical costume outside Narborough church, c. 1920.

A decorated horsedrawn dray in Enderby around 1940. Alf Cooper is on the left with Marion Elliott.

The Co-operative Jubilee Fête, Enderby, c. 1930. One of the Biggs family is driving the car.

Children in fancy dress at the annual Enderby Fête and Walk, in 1950.

The Enderby pageant, celebrating St John the Baptist, Enderby Wake, 24 June 1915.

Bunting is hung out for celebrations in Connery Lane, Enderby. They are possibly for the end of war celebrations in 1945.

A street party at The Nook, Enderby, celebrating the end of the Second World War in 1945.

When a King rode through Enderby. In 1895, King Khama of the Bamangwato Tribe in Bechuanaland (Botswana) visited Enderby to fulfil a promise to a teacher working in one of the missionary schools in the capital Palapye. Miss Alice Young, of Enderby, had been assured by the King that if he came to England he would pay a visit to the village. The King, accompanied by two chiefs, Sebele and Bathoen, came as part of the London Missionary Society's 100th anniversary celebrations. The visit was made a public holiday and after formal proceedings, at which he was presented with an illuminated address, the guests had a meal at the schoolrooms next to the chapel. Following this the party were shown around Enderby Hall and grounds by Captain Drummond and his family. The top hatted King Khama is seated with his back to the driver. On the carriage, from left to right: -?-, -?-, Thomas Young, King Khama, Chief Sebele, Chief Bathoen, Keautile, Willoughby, Simon Seisa, Revd G.H. Dickenson, William Young, -?-. Standing in front, -?-, George Gamble, Thomas Young and Harry Biggs, holding the illuminated address presented to the King by the local Good Templars.

Opposite above: A coronation party, Connery Lane, Mill Hill, in 1953.

Opposite below: A bus outing for senior citizens on Co-operative Street, Enderby, in 1954. Their destination was Skegness. Arthur Capers MBE stands to the right of the bus.

Left: The mother of Alice Young is seen here with King Khama, during his walkabout in Enderby.

Below left and right: Mr and Mrs William Young, parents of Miss Alice Young.

King Khama seated with the rest of the party during a civic dinner. The dinner was held at the school rooms, next to the Congregational chapel. Standing, left to right: Percy Young, Jane Young, Ellen Gamble, Elizabeth Young, Ezra Young, Revd G.A. Dickenson, Alice Gamble, George Gamble, Mary Ann Young, -?-. Seated, left to right: -?-, -?-, -?-, -?-, -?-, -?-, Willoughby, King Khama, Mary Young, held by William Young, -?-, Chief Sebele, Simon Seisa, Thomas Young, Mrs Young (Alice's mother), -?-, Tom Young, Mrs Tom Young and Elizabeth Young.

Eric Roderick Brook Drummond in the uniform of the Rifle Brigade, *c.* 1920.

The Drummond Family Coat of Arms. The Drummond family were key figures in Enderby parish and resided at Enderby Hall. Their ancestors can be traced to Edward I, King of England (1272–1301).

Seven

Transport, Trade and Industry

A steam lorry, operated by the Old Granite Co. Ltd, Enderby, c. 1905.

Cross Street, Enderby, during excavations for the laying of sewer pipes, *c.* 1890. The Nags Head public house is the building on the right. Just below the surface is solid rock. Faced with such conditions, the contractors called in the experts in such matters – the quarrymen.

Enderby Quarry, in 1877. The area was originally called First Hanging which was the name of the field. It later became known as Blaby Road Quarry.

Enderby Hill Quarry in 1910. Connery Lane runs across the top of the picture.

A group of Enderby quarry workers from the 1890s.

Kerb and sett makers, working outside their sheds, at Enderby Hill Quarry, in 1914.

Above: Enderby Hill Quarry, looking up towards Mill Hill, c. 1900. Quarrying began on Enderby Hill in 1863 when two families, the Rawsons and the Robsons, saw the potential for granite setts. Stone from here was regularly taken by horse and cart to Leicester Jail to be broken up by prisoners serving sentences of hard labour. Enderby Hill Quarry closed in 1936.

Right: Steam drilling at Enderby Hill Quarry, in 1905.

This Enderby and Stoney Stanton Granite Company steam cart was used for local deliveries c. 1910. Its maximum load was 7 tons 2 cwts.

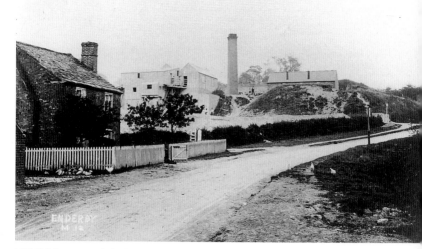

Mill Hill Quarry, Enderby, looking along the Desford Road towards Mill Hill around 1930.

An aerial view of Enderby Warren Quarry in 1957.

A 0-4-0 standard gauge saddle tank locomotive named 'Trot', at Enderby Warren Quarry, in 1940.

Drilling at the Warren Quarry, Enderby, in 1918.

A saddle tank steam locomotive named 'Elizabeth', at the Warren Enderby, in 1930. The driver is Tommy Peach. The engine operated on top of the quarry, shunting wagons of stone to the connection with the main line.

A group of quarry men working at the Warren in 1920. The quarry manager's house, which was called Pen-y Craig after a place in Wales, is visible in the distance through the trees.

The sett makers at Enderby Warren, in the 1940s.

Above: Diesel locomotives at Enderby Quarry, 1950s.

Left: The Enderby Quarry rail link belonging to the London North East Railway Company, c. 1960.

The transportation of a heavy transformer to the electricity sub-station along Mill Hill, passing under the now demolished quarry line railway bridge in 1991.

The Empire Stone Company, Narborough.
Thomas J. McDowell founded this company in Leicester in 1900, but moved to the Narborough site in 1901. On the payroll of the twenty-five men employed in May 1901, was C.K. Smith, grandfather of M.J.K. Smith, the famous England cricketer. C.K. Smith was to prove himself to be a valuable employee, through his experimental mixes of selected natural stone aggregate, white cement and powder pigments. An 'artificial' stone evolved bearing a remarkable likeness in both colour and texture to natural building stone such as Portland and Bath.

After the First World War, this type of reconstructed stone found increasing favour with architects, and the growth of the company was only temporarily halted by the depression of 1932. At this time 650 men were on the company's payroll. Some builders were still sceptical about the weathering properties of a man-made substitute for natural stone and used it only for heavy cornices which could be moulded at much less cost than mason stone. Examples of its use can be found in London on the Cumberland Hotel, Selfridges, Peter Robinson and Fortnum & Masons. Local examples of this post-war work can be seen at British Shoe Corporations Offices, Leicester and Next Offices, Enderby. Stone was also exported to all parts of the world and used as a cladding for buildings. The company ceased trading in 1994.

The Empire Stone Company Narborough, 1945. Bill Hunt was one of the last skilled carvers to work for the company. He is seen here working on a moulding.

Opposite above: The drawing office of the Empire Stone Company, Narborough, in 1986.

Opposite below: Here is Bert Graham working on a mould at the Empire Stone Company, in 1975. The mould is for a fountain base to be fitted in the cruise liner the 'Royal Princess'.

A pen and ink drawing of framework knitters at work in Enderby, dated 1899.

The stocking frame, used in framework knitting was invented by William Lee, a Nottinghamshire clergyman, in 1589, and was to have far-reaching consequences for the rural communities in Leicestershire. A man named William Iliffe is reputed to have introduced the first stocking frame into the county at Hinckley. The industry spread rapidly into what had been a mainly agricultural economy. The drawing, by Potts, illustrates the kind of machine that was used to produce the stockings made with these devices. The majority of frames were in the home or in a shed in the backyard. Only later did this developed into a more organised system where middlemen rented out space in purpose-built 'Frameshops' so that knitters could be paid for the actual work they produced. However they had to pay rent for the frames as well as for candles and coal for heating and lighting.

In 1844, a Royal Commission was appointed to inquire into the wages and conditions of framework knitters in Leicestershire, Nottinghamshire and Derbyshire. In the report were some particularly interesting testimonies by people who were engaged in the trade in Enderby. One of the framework knitters who was examined was Joseph Jayes who said: '...my means so far as sending a child to school are so limited that whatever education they receive must be from my own hands, and then I am so exhausted that I am obliged to go and lie down for an hour at a time at night. The wages of stocking making will not produce the necessary support to keep up a person's strength.'

The demise of the framework-knitting industry in rural areas was caused by two factors; firstly, The Education Act of 1870–1876 made school compulsory for children between the ages of five and fourteen. This prevented children from being used as cheap labour. More important, though, was the development of wider steam-powered frames which could not be accommodated in the small cottages. The use of steam power had a major effect on the domestic industry, and although the hand-frame did not die out until the First World War, the advent of centralized factories soon made it redundant.

A group of workers, possibly at the boot and shoe works in King Street, Enderby, c. 1900.

The boot and shoe trade had similar beginnings to the hosiery trade inasmuch as it started as a domestic industry, which then progressed to be factory based. By 1888 a lot of changes had taken place in the boot and shoe industry – mainly because of demand. The domestic trade still carried on, but factories were being built to cope with the increased demand.

One of the biggest manufacturers in this period was the Manchester-based Co-operative Wholesale Society, which had opened the West End boot and shoe factory in Duns Lane in Leicester in 1873. It is interesting to note that in 1874, the CWS factory in Leicester had so much work that: 'certain manufactures were given out at Enderby, a small village some four or five miles distant from Leicester – a room being rented for this purpose from Enderby Co-operative Society' (extract from 'The Story of the CWS' – Manchester Archives). No doubt labour was cheaper in rural areas.

To bring this operation under direct CWS control a small factory was built at King Street, in Enderby, in 1888. By 1890, there were 150 workers employed in this factory, and by 1900 there were three factories making boots and shoes in Enderby. These were the Co-operative works, Hopkins, Smith and Co. and William Young, shoe manufacturer, in King Street.

Enderby boot and shoe works. The factory was built in 1888. Prior to this, work was carried out from rooms in the village rented from the Enderby Co-operative Society.

A horse and carriage, transporting the bride and groom to the church – although the vicar appears to be conducting the ceremony during the ride, Enderby, c. 1920.

Above: Narborough railway station, looking south, in 1950.

Right: A passenger alights from a steam train at Narborough station, in 1949. Note the steps which were necessary because of the height of the carriage.

A view of the road between Narborough and Littlethorpe during severe flooding, *c.* 1940.

A double-decker bus at the corner of Coalpit Lane, Welford Place, *c.* 1930. Its destination was Welford Place in Leicester.

Right: Delivering milk by horse and cart in Enderby, *c.* 1920. The thatched cottage on the right is now Barclays Bank.

Below: An Enderby Co-op milkman poses for a photograph with his milk float, *c.* 1930.

A village outing in a charabanc, in the 1920s.

Opposite: The selling of the Wether.
This was an ancient custom said to have started in 1370, during the reign of Edward III, by John O'Gaunt, Duke of Lancaster and Earl of Leicester as they were journeying to Leicester from Market Bosworth *via* Ratby. The Duke saw several men in a field occupied in various athletic pursuits and they invited him to join in, and later to stay for music and dancing in the evening. Having enjoyed himself so much, he promised to give the men a plot of land, two acres in extent, called the 'Wether Then, each Whit Monday they were to ride from Ratby to the Nag's Head at Enderby, to 'sell' the Wether in the following way: After partaking of bread and cheese and ale, their leader was to declare the sale open. The land could not be sold for under four pounds, and nothing less than two pence would be accepted as a bid. A coin was to be passed around and only when the coin was in hand could a bid be made. When a complete circuit with the coin had been made without a bid the last bidder was declared the purchaser. The money obtained was to be taken to Leicester to pay for the meals to be provided by the caterers. On reaching Leicester, the whole assembly marched to St Mary de-Castro church, to hear a sermon preached on behalf of Trinity hospital in the Newark, which was founded by Henry, Earl of Lancaster. They would return to the inn for the meal provided for them. The rest of the day was to be spent in 'jollification' until the money was spent. In 1821, the rights of the Ratby men were disposed of, and the rights of the Wether were handed over to the people of Enderby. The conditions of sale were then somewhat altered. The people taking part in the sale paid one shilling, and shag tobacco was provided, with churchwarden pipes smoked during the sale. The custom was discontinued some years ago.